Virtual Reference Revolution

Integrating Virtual And Augmented Reality For Enhancing Library Services

Amelia Blackwell

Contents

1 Introduction to VR/AR in Libraries **5**
1.1 The Evolving Library Landscape 7
1.2 VR/AR Technologies Overview 9

2 Virtual Library Tours & Spaces **13**
2.1 Designing Immersive Library Experiences 15
2.2 3D Modeling and Virtual Environments 17
2.3 User Interaction and Navigation 18

3 Augmented Reality for Research & Discovery **21**
3.1 AR for Enhanced Catalog Searching 23
3.2 Interactive Displays and Exhibits 25
3.3 Overlaying Digital Content onto Physical Books 27
3.4 Integrating AR with Library Databases 30
3.5 Accessibility and Inclusivity with AR 31

4 Virtual Reference Services **35**
4.1 Remote Assistance via VR/AR 37
4.2 Training and Education for Librarians 40

5 VR/AR for Digital Literacy Programs **43**
5.1 Integrating VR/AR into Workshops 46
5.2 Gamification and Interactive Learning 48
5.3 Assessing Learning Outcomes 50

6 Challenges and Opportunities **53**
6.1 Technological Barriers and Costs 55
6.2 Accessibility and Inclusivity 57
6.3 Privacy and Security Concerns 59

7 Future Trends and Conclusion **63**
7.1 The Metaverse and Libraries 65
7.2 Emerging Technologies and their Impact 67
7.3 The Future of Library Services 69
7.4 Ethical Considerations 70
7.5 Next Steps 72

1 Introduction to VR/AR in Libraries

Libraries, once solely repositories of physical books, are evolving. They are becoming vibrant hubs of digital learning and community engagement, and VR/AR technologies are pivotal in this transformation. Understanding the potential of these technologies is crucial for modern librarianship, driving innovation and enriching the user experience.

The shift towards digital resources demands a parallel evolution in service delivery. No longer limited by physical space, libraries can leverage VR to create immersive virtual tours of their collections, providing access to users regardless of geographical location. This expansion of accessibility is transformative for individuals with mobility limitations or those in remote areas. Imagine a student in a rural community, able to explore the shelves of a major research library from their home, accessing resources otherwise unattainable.

Augmented reality offers a different, yet equally powerful, avenue for enhancing library services. AR overlays digital information onto the real world, creating interactive experiences that enrich the user's interaction with physical materials. This could manifest in a myriad of ways, for example, pointing a smartphone at a book to reveal its reviews, related articles, or even a 3D model of the book's setting if it's a historical fiction. Such interactive layers turn passive browsing into an active, engaging, and insightful learning experience. This is particularly beneficial for research-oriented users seeking to contextualize their study.

Consider the benefits for researchers studying ancient civilizations. By pointing their AR-enabled device at a relevant artifact or book, they might view interactive timelines, 3D reconstructions of ancient cities, or even listen to recordings of related lectures—all within the library's physical walls, seamlessly integrating digital and physical resources. Such experiences are not just entertaining; they enhance comprehension, spark curiosity, and fundamentally change how we learn and explore.

Implementing VR/AR in libraries requires careful planning and strategic integration. Librarians need adequate training to understand and use these tools effectively. This includes learning how to create engaging virtual tours, designing intuitive user interfaces for AR applications, and addressing potential technical difficulties. Moreover, it demands a proactive approach towards addressing accessibility concerns—ensuring that VR/AR services are usable for users with disabilities. Inclusive design is not optional; it's a fundamental aspect of integrating these new technologies responsibly and effectively.

Financial constraints might initially present a hurdle. The cost of acquiring VR/AR equipment and software, combined with the need for staff training, can be substantial. However, it's crucial to consider the long-term return on investment. Increased accessibility, enhanced learning experiences, and the potential to attract new user demographics can justify the upfront costs. Exploring funding opportunities, grants, and collaborative partnerships could help libraries overcome these financial barriers.

Furthermore, privacy and security concerns need thorough consideration. VR/AR applications often collect user data, raising questions regarding data protection and responsible use. Libraries must establish clear data privacy policies, ensuring user consent and transparent data handling practices. Transparency and user control over data are paramount, fostering trust and encouraging wider adoption. Successfully navigating these concerns through robust policies and user education will be essential for building confidence and establishing a positive user experience.

The future of libraries is inextricably linked to the adoption and integration of new technologies. While challenges remain, the potential benefits of VR/AR are immense. By carefully addressing these challenges, proactively planning for implementation, and prioritizing user accessibility and privacy, libraries can harness the power of VR/AR to transform how they serve their communities, fostering a dynamic, engaging, and inclusive learning environment for all. The transformation is underway, and the forward-thinking library will be at the forefront, shaping the future of information access and learning. The opportunities presented are too significant to ignore.

1.1 The Evolving Library Landscape

Libraries, once solely repositories of physical books, are undergoing a profound metamorphosis. The digital revolution has already reshaped how we access information; now, virtual and augmented reality are poised to redefine the very experience of the library itself. This shift isn't merely about adopting new technologies; it's about fundamentally reimagining the library's role in society. We are moving beyond a space for solely accessing information to a hub for immersive learning, dynamic engagement, and community building.

The traditional model, with its rows of shelves and hushed silence, is being challenged. The evolving library landscape requires librarians to embrace new skills and approaches, to understand the possibilities of VR and AR, and to integrate them seamlessly into existing services. This isn't about replacing the physical library; rather, it's about augmenting its capabilities and expanding its reach to those who may not have easy physical access. Think of it as the next logical step in library evolution, building upon past innovations like online catalogs and digital databases.

Consider the potential of virtual library tours. Imagine users exploring historical archives from their homes, virtually navigating labyrinthine stacks, or experiencing a museum exhibit without leaving their seats. This expands accessibility exponentially, reaching patrons with physical limitations or geographical barriers. Further, creating immersive virtual spaces allows for curated experiences, highlighting specific collections or themes in ways that simply aren't possible in a physical setting. The possibilities for engagement are limitless, transforming the passive experience of browsing into an active and explorative journey.

This shift necessitates a reassessment of librarian roles. Librarians will be less curators of physical spaces and more designers of digital experiences. They will need to master new tools and techniques, from 3D modeling software to user interface design. Furthermore, a deep understanding of the educational and psychological impact of virtual and augmented environments becomes essential in order to create truly effective and engaging experiences for library users. This means embracing new forms of professional development and embracing collaboration across disciplines—with tech developers, educators, and even artists—to fully leverage these technologies.

The successful integration of VR/AR hinges on user experience. Intuitive navigation, compelling visuals, and informative content are crucial. Poorly designed interfaces will quickly lead to user frustration, undermining the technology's potential. Therefore, usability testing and iterative design are paramount. We must prioritize creating accessible virtual environments, considering the needs of users with disabilities, ensuring that VR/AR enhances rather than hinders inclusivity. This needs to be built into the design process from the very start, not as an afterthought.

But this technological revolution is not without its hurdles. The cost of implementing VR/AR technology can be substantial, requiring significant investments in hardware, software, and training. Moreover, ensuring digital equity is crucial. The library's role in providing access to information and technology for all must be maintained and enhanced in this new digital landscape. We must proactively address potential biases in VR/AR content and work towards ensuring equitable access for all members of the community, regardless of socioeconomic status or technological literacy. This also includes robust consideration of privacy and security concerns.

Looking ahead, the integration of VR/AR in libraries promises to be transformative. It opens doors to entirely new possibilities for education, research, and community engagement. As technology evolves, so too will the library's capacity to deliver innovative and engaging services, making it a truly dynamic and inclusive space for all. The future library isn't merely a building; it's a network of physical and virtual spaces, seamlessly integrated to serve the evolving needs of its community. We are on the cusp of a new era for libraries, one that embraces technology to enhance and amplify the essential services libraries provide. The challenge for us now is to navigate this landscape thoughtfully, responsibly, and inclusively.

1.2 VR/AR Technologies Overview

Virtual Reality (VR) immerses users in completely computer-generated environments, offering a sense of presence and interaction unlike any other medium. Imagine a user exploring a historical library in ancient Rome, walking amongst towering bookshelves filled with scrolls, or participating in a virtual book club meeting with individuals from around the globe—all from the comfort of their own home. This level of engagement fosters deeper understanding and appreciation for both the content and the context. The technology's potential extends far beyond mere entertainment; it offers powerful tools for education, research, and collaboration, especially when integrated with carefully designed library services.

Augmented Reality (AR), conversely, overlays digital information onto the real world, enhancing our perception of reality. Think of a user pointing their smartphone at a physical book, instantly receiving access to related digital resources – reviews, author biographies, related articles, and even interactive 3D models pertaining to the book's subject matter. AR doesn't replace the physical experience; it enriches it, transforming a simple library visit into an interactive learning adventure. The ability to seamlessly blend digital and physical worlds creates unique opportunities for discovery and engagement, especially for patrons who might be intimidated by fully immersive virtual environments. Moreover, this technology can be implemented relatively easily in many existing library settings.

The core difference lies in their immersion levels. VR fully submerges the user, creating a separate reality, while AR enhances the existing one. Both, however, share a common goal: to enhance engagement and understanding. The choice between VR and AR for specific library applications will depend on several factors, including the target audience, the specific learning objectives, and the available budget and technical resources. For example, while a virtual tour of a historical archive might benefit from the complete immersion of VR, an AR application overlaying digital information onto physical books could be more practical for daily library use.

Consider the possibilities for remote reference services. VR could enable librarians to provide personalized assistance to patrons regardless of physical location, creating a sense of virtual proximity and facilitating a more natural, interactive dialogue. Imagine a librarian guiding a patron through a research database, virtually pointing to specific entries and offering personalized advice—all within a shared, immersive virtual space. This would overcome the limitations of traditional remote reference methods, offering a much more engaging and effective alternative. However, factors like network speed and user technical skills will need careful consideration.

The potential integration of VR/AR with library databases is particularly exciting. Imagine searching a library catalog not through a flat screen, but through a three-dimensional interactive environment where users can explore the catalog visually, sorting results intuitively and selecting items that are relevant to their query through intuitive gestures. The experience would be far more engaging and intuitive than traditional methods, making the search process itself a more enjoyable and productive learning opportunity for users. This requires thoughtful consideration of the user experience and careful design of database interfaces.

Furthermore, the potential of VR/AR extends beyond research and discovery. These technologies can be harnessed to create engaging digital literacy programs. Imagine gamified learning environments where users navigate virtual libraries, solve puzzles to locate information, or interact with virtual librarians who guide them through information literacy concepts. This interactive, immersive approach could make learning more engaging and effective than traditional methods. Assessment of the learning outcomes would also require careful consideration, utilizing methods tailored to the specific virtual environments. Successful implementation also necessitates proper training for library staff in using and supporting these technologies.

Cost, technical expertise, and accessibility are significant hurdles. The initial investment in VR/AR hardware and software can be substantial. Moreover, ensuring that these technologies are accessible to all patrons, regardless of their technological literacy or physical abilities, is crucial. This includes considerations for users with visual, auditory, or motor impairments, requiring careful design to ensure inclusivity. Privacy and security are also important considerations, requiring robust safeguards to protect user data and maintain a safe virtual environment. The successful implementation of VR/AR in libraries requires careful planning, adequate funding, and ongoing training for staff. Despite these challenges, the potential benefits of VR/AR for transforming library services are immense, promising a more engaging, interactive, and accessible future for libraries and their patrons alike.

2 Virtual Library Tours & Spaces

Creating a compelling virtual library tour requires careful planning and execution. Think of it as designing an experience, not just a digital space. The user's journey should be intuitive and engaging, guiding them smoothly through the virtual collection and highlighting key features. This necessitates a deep understanding of user experience (UX) design principles, ensuring ease of navigation and a captivating visual aesthetic. We need to avoid overwhelming users with information overload, instead opting for a carefully curated selection of highlights and interactive elements. Imagine walking into a real library—you wouldn't be bombarded with every single book; you'd be drawn to specific areas or displays. Replicate this feeling within the virtual environment.

The technical side, however, is just as crucial. 3D modeling software, like Blender or SketchUp, becomes your primary tool. Detailed models of the physical library, or the creation of a completely new virtual space, depend on your goals. Accuracy in representing existing architecture offers a sense of familiarity and credibility, while a newly designed virtual space offers more freedom to create immersive learning experiences. For example, a historical library could be replicated to its exact form, allowing users to explore periods of time or even interact with digital versions of historical books. Regardless of your approach, ensuring the virtual environment performs smoothly, avoiding lag or glitches, is paramount for a positive user experience. Optimized models and efficient coding practices are therefore essential.

Effective user interaction is the key to a successful virtual library tour. Intuitive navigation is paramount; users shouldn't be wrestling with complicated controls. Consider incorporating straightforward methods such as directional arrows, clickable hotspots, and even virtual avatars that guide users. The incorporation of interactive elements further enhances the user's experience. Clickable books that open to digital pages, interactive exhibits with embedded videos and audio components, and virtual tours led by a digital guide can all add to the engagement. Remember that the interactive elements must be relevant and contribute meaningfully to the virtual tour, not just serve as empty decorations. The use of interactive 3D models of artifacts or historical objects also provides an engaging and relevant experience for users.

Accessibility must be a top priority. Your virtual library should be accessible to all users, regardless of physical limitations or disabilities. This involves careful consideration of color contrast, font size, and the inclusion of alternative text for screen readers. Closed captions should accompany any audio content, and keyboard navigation should be supported for those unable to use a mouse. Consider adding various customization options such as adjusting field of view and zoom levels for visually impaired users. Accessibility should not be an afterthought, but an integral part of the design process. Designing for inclusivity ensures that everyone can participate and benefit from this immersive learning environment. This might involve working with accessibility experts during the development process to ensure the virtual library meets accessibility standards, particularly if you are creating virtual libraries based on real libraries that already meet WCAG guidelines.

Beyond the initial design, ongoing maintenance and updates are essential to keep the virtual library fresh and relevant. New exhibits, books, and interactive elements can be added periodically. Regular testing and user feedback sessions are crucial to identify areas for improvement and ensure the experience remains engaging. A vibrant virtual library is a living space, constantly evolving to meet the needs of its users. This iterative process ensures that the virtual library continues to serve as a dynamic and valuable resource, continually adapting to current needs and providing a truly enriching experience for users. Monitoring user statistics and engagement metrics helps assess the success of the virtual library and inform future updates and improvements. Regular upgrades to the technology underpinning the virtual environment, such as incorporating new rendering techniques for improved graphics or integrating new VR/AR capabilities, will keep the library experience modern and appealing. Continuous improvement is essential.

2.1 Designing Immersive Library Experiences

Creating a truly immersive virtual library experience requires careful consideration of several key elements. The goal isn't simply to replicate a physical space digitally; it's to build something that transcends the limitations of the physical, offering richer, more engaging interactions with information. Think about how users will interact with the space; intuitive navigation is paramount. Clear visual cues, easily accessible menus, and consistent controls are crucial for a positive user experience. Avoid overwhelming users with excessive detail or complex interfaces. Simplicity and ease of use should always be prioritized. Consider incorporating haptic feedback for a more realistic and interactive experience, allowing users to "feel" the textures of virtual books or the weight of virtual objects. This can add a surprising layer of depth to the digital experience.

Successful virtual library design hinges on compelling visual aesthetics. The virtual environment should be visually appealing, inviting, and reflective of the library's brand and mission. High-resolution textures, realistic lighting, and meticulously crafted models are essential for creating a sense of place and immersion. Avoid using jarring color palettes or overly simplistic designs. The space should feel inviting and comfortable, encouraging exploration and interaction. Don't underestimate the power of ambient sounds; subtly incorporated background music or realistic environmental sounds can greatly enhance the overall experience, creating a more relaxing and immersive atmosphere. The right soundscape can significantly improve the mood and enhance focus.

Beyond the aesthetics, the functionality of your virtual library is crucial. Consider the different ways users might interact with the information within. Will they be able to browse virtual shelves, select and "open" virtual books, or engage with interactive exhibits? The possibilities are vast, and the design should support a diverse range of interactions. For example, integrating virtual reality headsets could allow users to explore a 360-degree view of the library or even step inside a virtual archive. This level of immersion can transform the way users engage with information, making learning more memorable and accessible. Thorough planning and testing are essential to ensure a seamless and intuitive user experience, enabling effortless access to information and resources.
Think about accessibility. Virtual library spaces should be designed to be inclusive, accessible to users with diverse needs and abilities. This might involve incorporating features such as text-to-speech, adjustable font sizes, and alternative navigation methods. Consider also color contrast ratios and the use of visual cues that cater to individuals with various visual impairments. Implementing closed captions for videos or audio guides is equally important. Prioritizing accessibility is more than just compliance; it's about ensuring that everyone can benefit from the immersive learning opportunities a virtual library offers. It's about building a genuinely inclusive environment for all. This demonstrates the library's commitment to inclusivity and ensures its virtual spaces remain welcoming and accessible for all visitors.
Finally, the long-term success of a virtual library depends on ongoing evaluation and improvement. Regularly collect user feedback through surveys, usability testing, and analytics data. This feedback will provide invaluable insights into what's working well and what needs improvement. Use this data to refine your design, enhance functionality, and ensure your virtual library remains a relevant and engaging resource for your users. Continuous improvement is key to keeping the experience fresh, engaging, and meeting the evolving needs of the library's community. Remember, a successful virtual library is not a static entity; it's a dynamic and responsive space that constantly adapts and grows.

2.2 3D Modeling and Virtual Environments

Creating realistic and engaging virtual library spaces requires a solid understanding of 3D modeling software. Blender, a free and open-source option, provides a powerful suite of tools for beginners and experts alike. Familiarize yourself with its interface, focusing on the key functionalities for modeling, texturing, and lighting. Start with simple shapes, gradually increasing complexity as you master the basics. Experiment with different modeling techniques, such as extrusion, beveling, and sculpting, to create diverse elements for your virtual library. Remember, practice is key; don't be afraid to experiment and learn from your mistakes.

Next, consider the library's architecture. Will your virtual space mimic an existing building, or will it be a completely original design? Either way, accurate measurements are crucial for creating a believable environment. If modeling an existing building, utilize architectural plans or conduct on-site measurements. For original designs, sketch out your ideas first, ensuring the layout is functional and aesthetically pleasing. Think about the flow of the space, placement of bookshelves, reading areas, and other essential features.

Texturing adds realism and visual appeal. High-quality textures significantly enhance the immersive experience. You can create your own textures using image editing software or utilize freely available resources online, remembering to always respect copyright. Experiment with different materials to create a variety of surfaces—wood, metal, fabric, and more—to add depth and visual interest to your virtual library. Pay close attention to detail; subtle textures can significantly improve the overall aesthetic quality.

Lighting is just as crucial as modeling and texturing. Effective lighting can create atmosphere and highlight key features. Experiment with different light sources—ambient, directional, and point lights—to achieve the desired effect. Consider the time of day and the type of lighting you wish to simulate. Natural lighting can add realism, while artificial lighting can be used to create specific moods. Proper lighting will make your virtual library feel more inviting and realistic.

Once your model is complete, you'll need to export it into a game engine, such as Unity or Unreal Engine, to create the interactive virtual environment. These engines provide tools for adding user interaction, navigation, and other interactive elements. Learning the basics of these engines is vital, even if you outsource the final integration. Understanding the process will enable you to communicate effectively with developers and ensure the final product meets your vision.

Remember to prioritize user experience. Intuitive navigation is paramount. Consider employing common interface elements such as clear signage, easily identifiable waypoints, and responsive controls. Testing your virtual library with potential users is also crucial to identify any usability issues early on. Gathering feedback and iterating on the design based on user testing will result in a more accessible and enjoyable experience for all.

Finally, explore different software solutions. While Blender is an excellent free option, other commercial software packages such as 3ds Max or Maya offer advanced features. The choice depends on your budget, technical skills, and specific project needs. Research the strengths and weaknesses of different software packages to make an informed decision. Consider collaborating with 3D modeling professionals if your expertise is limited; their assistance can significantly streamline the process. The goal is to create a user-friendly and visually appealing virtual library that enriches the user experience.

2.3 User Interaction and Navigation

Effective navigation is paramount in a successful virtual library experience. Clunky controls or confusing interfaces can quickly derail even the most meticulously crafted 3D environment. Imagine a user struggling to find a specific book in a vast virtual collection, becoming frustrated and abandoning the experience entirely. This is precisely why intuitive user interaction is crucial. Consider employing clear visual cues, such as highlighted pathways or directional arrows, to guide users through the

space. Simple, consistent icons representing actions like "open," "zoom," or "select" will dramatically improve usability. Remember to design for accessibility. Users with motor impairments might require alternative input methods, such as voice commands or eye-tracking technology.
A well-designed virtual library should feel natural and intuitive. Think about the physical experience of navigating a real library; users seamlessly transition between browsing shelves, consulting the catalog, and finding seating areas. Your virtual library should reflect this natural flow. Avoid overwhelming users with too much information at once. Instead, provide clear pathways and options for exploration, allowing users to discover features gradually. Think layered information. Initially display an overview of the library, then allow users to zoom into specific areas or collections as they choose. This staged approach enhances the sense of discovery and prevents cognitive overload.
Intuitive interaction goes beyond simple point-and-click mechanics. Consider incorporating gestures for common actions, such as grabbing and moving virtual objects or rotating books to view their covers. The use of realistic physics, allowing books to stack realistically or fall to the ground when dropped, adds another layer of immersion. However, balance realism with functionality. Too much realism can slow down the application and frustrate users. The objective is to create a compelling experience, not a perfect simulation. We want a functional system that will not require too much computing power.
Developing a robust search function is equally critical. Users should be able to quickly and easily find specific books, journals, or other resources. A simple text-based search, coupled with advanced filtering options based on metadata like subject, author, and publication date, is a must. Consider visual representations of search results, with 3D book covers or thumbnails that users can click to open the virtual book. Moreover, this visual search can dramatically reduce processing time needed for browsing, speeding the process for those looking for a particular work, allowing for greater ease of finding materials. This allows for more rapid information retrieval in a space where the library can customize the retrieval of materials.
Personalization is key to enhancing user engagement. If a user has saved

previous searches or frequently accesses certain collections, the virtual library could proactively offer relevant recommendations. This personalized approach not only improves efficiency but also provides a more tailored and enjoyable experience. Consider integrating user profiles to store preferences and customize the interface to each user's needs. This personal touch will make the virtual library feel more welcoming and engaging, inviting users to return again and again. This allows the user to access their preferred materials and allows the administrator to track usage and trends.

Remember to constantly test and iterate based on user feedback. Collect data on user behavior, such as navigation patterns, search queries, and dwell times, to identify areas for improvement. A/B testing of different interface designs can be instrumental. A user survey or interview may provide invaluable insight. Iterative development is crucial to ensuring that the virtual library remains user-friendly, engaging, and effective. Therefore, regular feedback from testers and users should be part of the design process.

Finally, consider the overall aesthetic of the virtual environment. A well-designed space that evokes a sense of calm and focus can significantly improve the user experience. Natural lighting, comfortable seating arrangements, and attention to details such as book shelving and decor can make a significant difference. It's all part of establishing a pleasant atmosphere and improving users' comfort level within the digital library space. This is all essential for creating a positive and enjoyable interaction. A virtual library can greatly improve users' engagement, and should be designed to do that in the best way possible.

3 Augmented Reality for Research & Discovery

Imagine a student researching the history of the Roman Empire. Instead of sifting through countless pages, they could use an AR app to overlay 3D models of Roman artifacts directly onto the pages of a relevant book, seeing the actual size and detail of a discovered coin or a fragment of a mosaic. This isn't science fiction; it's the power of augmented reality in research and discovery. This technology allows for a richer, more engaging, and intuitive learning process. It transforms the static pages of a book into a dynamic window into the past.

For librarians, AR offers a powerful tool to enhance the research experience. Consider the possibilities of an AR overlay on a library catalog search result. The user doesn't simply see a list of books; instead, the app could project a 360-degree view of the book's cover, showcasing its spine and detailing its contents via additional information such as images of illustrations or maps contained within the text. It could even provide a short video preview of the book's contents in the same place they are researching. This level of detail allows for more informed decisions.

Interactive exhibits become vastly more engaging using AR. Imagine walking through a library exhibit about the history of printing, and as you look at a Gutenberg Bible replica, your AR device overlays a detailed animation of the printing process itself. It shows the individual steps in 3D, complete with the sounds of the machinery, and even allows you to rotate and zoom on individual components. Such engaging visual storytelling captivates and imparts knowledge more effectively than simple text panels ever could.

The integration of AR with existing library databases can profoundly alter how research is conducted. Instead of passively searching through records, users could utilize AR to explore the database visually. Imagine a researcher searching for articles on climate change. An AR app could present the search results not as a list, but as a dynamic network of interconnected nodes, each representing an article. The size of the nodes could indicate citation frequency, and the connections between them could highlight relationships between various research papers, enabling a far more holistic and intuitive grasp of the research landscape. This visual representation makes understanding the relationships between different works of research far easier and faster than a simple list ever could.

Accessibility is a critical consideration in any technological advancement. This is why AR technology in libraries must be designed with accessibility in mind. For visually impaired users, AR could offer haptic feedback or audio descriptions of the overlaid digital content. For those with hearing impairments, clear visual cues and text alternatives should be provided. This inclusive design ensures that the benefits of AR technology extend to all patrons, regardless of their abilities. The aim should be to provide a rich and accessible experience for all, regardless of their background and abilities.

The development and implementation of AR in libraries are not without their challenges. The initial investment in hardware and software can be substantial, requiring careful budgeting and planning. Moreover, training library staff to effectively use and support AR technology is crucial. Ongoing professional development is essential to keep up with the rapid advancements in AR technology, making sure to find the right balance between practicality and innovation. Finally, addressing potential concerns related to data privacy and security will be paramount, striking the balance between innovation and secure use of sensitive data is key. Planning ahead and adapting accordingly is key.

However, the potential benefits of AR far outweigh these challenges. It offers a transformative opportunity for libraries to enhance their services and become even more indispensable resources for their communities. It's about making research more engaging, accessible, and ultimately, more successful. Augmented reality is not just a technological advancement; it's a pathway to a richer, more interactive, and ultimately, more fulfilling research experience. This is why the implementation of AR in libraries is not just an option; it's a necessary step towards the future of learning and discovery. Through forward thinking and careful implementation, libraries can leverage AR to revolutionize how their patrons access and interact with information.

3.1 AR for Enhanced Catalog Searching

Imagine walking through your library's catalog, not via a screen, but with a pair of AR glasses. Instead of endless scrolling, relevant book covers appear superimposed onto the physical shelves, dynamically updating as you refine your search. This isn't science fiction; it's the potential of AR for enhanced catalog searching, offering a revolutionary user experience. This enhanced search method transforms the often frustrating process of finding specific items into an intuitive and engaging adventure. A truly interactive experience increases user satisfaction and encourages exploration beyond their initial search terms.

This chapter will help you understand how to implement such a system within your library. Firstly, consider the technology itself. Selecting appropriate AR hardware is crucial. Lightweight headsets with good battery life are essential for prolonged use. Furthermore, robust software capable of seamlessly integrating with your existing library management system (LMS) is vital. This integration isn't simply about displaying cover art; it's about pulling real-time data – availability, location, reviews – and presenting it in a clear and accessible manner. This requires a significant investment in both hardware and software, but remember the return on investment lies in improved user satisfaction, increased resource utilization, and an enhanced library image.

The implementation process needs careful planning. Start with a pilot program, testing the AR system in a small section of your library. This allows you to identify and resolve any technological glitches before rolling it out across the entire collection. User feedback is paramount at this stage; solicit opinions from library patrons, paying particular attention to their comfort levels with the technology and their perceptions of its effectiveness. This feedback will inform refinements and ultimately influence the long-term success of your AR implementation. Don't underestimate the importance of simple, intuitive user interfaces; user-friendliness directly correlates with adoption rates.

Training your staff is another critical component. Librarians need to understand the technical aspects of the AR system and its integration with the existing library systems. Beyond the technical expertise, they should also be trained on how to assist patrons in effectively using the AR interface. Consider providing hands-on workshops for your staff to ensure they're confident in troubleshooting common issues and providing effective support to your patrons. This investment in training creates a knowledgeable support team capable of navigating and assisting users. Remember, successful technology integration rests as much on staff training as it does on technological choices.

Beyond the immediate implementation, you should also plan for ongoing maintenance and updates. Software needs regular updates to incorporate new features, bug fixes, and security patches. AR technology is constantly evolving; your system should adapt to new possibilities and improvements. This ongoing commitment to maintenance ensures the long-term sustainability and effectiveness of your AR-enhanced catalog. The cost of maintenance, however, should be factored into the overall budget of the project from the outset. Don't be afraid to request additional funding for both the initial deployment and ongoing maintenance, making sure you can showcase the benefits of the AR system as a justification.

Consider accessibility as a critical aspect of your AR system. Ensure your design caters to diverse learning styles and physical limitations. Features such as voice control and adjustable font sizes may be necessary for some users. Furthermore, consider offering both AR-based and traditional methods for catalog searching to accommodate users who may not feel comfortable using the AR technology. The aim is to enhance the library experience for all, not just a select few. Consider working with your patrons who have accessibility needs during the development phase, ensuring diverse representation in the implementation and design of the AR system.

Finally, the success of AR-enhanced catalog searching depends not only on the technology itself but also on the integration strategy. Consider how it fits within your overall library mission and goals. This technology is a tool; its effectiveness hinges on how it's incorporated into your existing workflows and user services. Its role is to enhance, not replace, existing systems. By strategically integrating AR with the library's current services and user experience, you ensure a smooth transition and seamless adoption amongst your patrons. Measure your success not just by technology adoption but by its contribution to improved user satisfaction and increased resource utilization.

3.2 Interactive Displays and Exhibits

Interactive displays and exhibits offer a powerful way to engage library patrons and enhance their research experience. Imagine walking into a library and encountering a holographic projection of a historical manuscript, allowing you to examine its details up close without handling the fragile original. This is the potential of augmented reality (AR) in a library setting. Such interactive elements can transform static displays into dynamic learning opportunities, making information accessible and engaging in ways traditional methods cannot. The key is careful planning and execution to ensure the technology seamlessly integrates with the library environment and patron experience.

Consider the possibilities for interactive timelines, where visitors can tap a date on a large touchscreen and be presented with relevant images, videos, and primary source documents. This approach creates a more intuitive and engaging narrative than a simple text-based display. By using multi-sensory experiences like sound effects and haptic feedback, the timeline could become even more immersive, leaving a lasting impact on the users and making them actively participate in the learning process. The possibilities are endless, allowing librarians to showcase unique collections and historical context in new, captivating ways.

Successful interactive exhibits require more than just flashy technology. They need careful consideration of the user experience. Navigation should be intuitive, the information presented should be clear and concise, and the overall design should be visually appealing and accessible to all users. Usability testing is essential to ensure that the exhibit is actually engaging and informative. For example, a poorly designed interface could lead to frustrated users who fail to interact with the displays and therefore miss the intended learning experience. Furthermore, a successful experience means planning the content with accessibility in mind for people with sensory processing differences.

Think about integrating QR codes into existing physical exhibits. Patrons can scan the codes with their smartphones or tablets to access additional information, such as high-resolution images, audio recordings, or 3D models. This approach complements physical exhibits rather than replacing them, expanding their capabilities and providing a richer learning experience. It also leverages the technology that people already have, ensuring maximum accessibility and ease of use, without requiring library visitors to download any new application or software. This simple strategy greatly increases the potential value of the resources already available in the physical space.

Beyond simple information delivery, interactive displays can facilitate collaborative learning. Imagine a touchscreen table that allows multiple users to work together on a research project, sharing annotations and notes in real-time. Such applications could encourage group activities and project-based learning, transforming the library into a hub for collaborative engagement. This interactive approach makes the learning experience far more active and collaborative and stimulates engagement with the materials and each other. Similarly, collaborative digital displays can encourage users to leave comments or suggestions on the information displayed which can then be curated by the librarian.

Designing interactive exhibits requires collaboration between librarians, technology specialists, and exhibit designers. This team approach ensures that the exhibits are both informative and engaging, incorporating both educational content and practical design expertise. Such a collaboration combines technological skills with an understanding of library collections and patron needs to develop dynamic and educational resources. This collaborative approach to design and maintenance is paramount to effective display implementation. The result will be a more effective and successful learning environment for the library's users.

The cost of implementing interactive displays and exhibits can be a significant factor. However, there are options available for libraries with limited budgets. Open-source software and affordable hardware can be used to create engaging exhibits without breaking the bank. Furthermore, many organizations offer grants and funding opportunities specifically for library technology projects. Librarians should actively seek these opportunities to help make the use of modern technology within their libraries possible and sustainable. It is important to think about budgeting carefully, planning which technologies to start with and ensuring that any chosen technology is feasible to maintain both technologically and financially.

Finally, remember that the purpose of interactive displays is to enhance the library experience. They should be carefully integrated into the library's overall collection strategy and educational goals. Regular evaluation and feedback from patrons are essential to ensure that the displays remain relevant, engaging, and effective. Continuous user feedback allows libraries to adapt and modify exhibits based on patron usage and opinions. This constant engagement allows the library to stay up-to-date with visitor needs, ensuring the exhibits remain dynamic and relevant. Ultimately, the goal is to create a more dynamic and engaging learning environment for all patrons.

3.3 Overlaying Digital Content onto Physical Books

Imagine holding a centuries-old book, its pages whispering tales of forgotten times. Now, imagine those same pages coming alive with interactive annotations, 3D models popping up to illustrate historical contexts, or even videos playing directly on the page, seamlessly integrated into the physical experience. This is the power of overlaying digital content onto physical books using augmented reality (AR). It's not merely about enhancing the book; it's about revolutionizing how we interact with knowledge.

This chapter delves into the practical applications of this technology within a library setting, focusing on implementation strategies and potential benefits. We will explore the different software and hardware required, addressing compatibility issues and potential challenges early on. Successfully implementing AR overlays requires a careful consideration of both the technological and logistical aspects, and we'll guide you through each step.

The selection of appropriate AR software is crucial. Several platforms offer varying levels of functionality and integration capabilities. Some are designed for simple image recognition and text overlays, while others facilitate complex 3D model rendering and interactive elements. Your choice will depend on the complexity of the digital content you plan to integrate and your budget constraints. Thorough research is needed, comparing features, user-friendliness, and long-term support offered by each provider. Remember to also consider the scalability of the chosen platform; it should be adaptable as your collection and needs evolve. Don't overlook the importance of a user-friendly interface, both for librarians managing the system and for patrons interacting with it.

Hardware compatibility is another significant hurdle to consider. AR experiences require specific devices, whether it's specialized AR glasses, tablets, or even smartphones. Ensure your chosen technology is compatible with the devices you intend to make available for your patrons. You will want to create a cost-effective approach to providing the equipment needed to access these enriched book experiences. Exploring options like shared devices in designated areas or creating a loan program for compatible tablets can help address the cost barrier.

Beyond the technical aspects, planning is essential. Before you start overlaying digital content, consider the overall user experience. Intuitive navigation is key; patrons shouldn't be struggling to find the digital enhancements. Well-designed overlays will seamlessly integrate with the book's physical form, enhancing the reading experience without disrupting the flow. Consider also the potential for accessibility features such as audio descriptions and adjustable text size for diverse audiences. Accessibility should be at the forefront of your design process.

Furthermore, think about how these digital enhancements can enrich the existing research process. For instance, you might overlay relevant scholarly articles, primary source materials, or expert commentary directly onto the physical pages of a historical text. This allows researchers to move effortlessly between the original source and supporting materials, enriching their understanding and research productivity. The potential for educational enrichment is tremendous, particularly for subjects requiring hands-on experience. Integrating interactive maps, 3D models, and virtual tours directly into textbooks can bring historical events, scientific concepts, or geographic locations to life in a truly engaging way.

The successful implementation of AR overlays requires thorough training. Librarians need to be familiar with the software, hardware, and troubleshooting procedures to provide assistance to patrons. Invest in comprehensive training programs to equip your staff with the necessary skills to confidently manage and support this technology. Regular workshops and refresher courses are also crucial to keep your team abreast of updates and new functionalities. Effective training is key to maximizing the benefits of the technology and ensuring a smooth user experience.

Finally, consider the long-term sustainability of your project. Technology evolves rapidly, so choose a system that can be updated and maintained over time. Develop strategies for data backup and disaster recovery to protect your valuable digital content. Regular audits of the system, software updates, and staff training are vital to ensure the longevity and effectiveness of the AR overlay program. The longevity and successful implementation of your program will be directly correlated to your commitment to continuous improvement. Therefore, planning for long-term support is critical for the overall success of your library's initiative.

3.4 Integrating AR with Library Databases

Imagine a student needing information on the French Revolution. Instead of navigating complex library databases, they could simply point their smartphone at a relevant section of a history textbook. An augmented reality overlay, powered by integrated library databases, could instantly display related primary source documents, relevant encyclopedia entries, and even 3D models of significant historical sites, all within the context of their physical book. This enhanced research experience, seamlessly blending the physical and digital, offers a new level of engagement and depth. The technology goes beyond simple annotations; it contextualizes the information, creating a dynamic learning environment.

This integration isn't merely about convenience; it's about enriching the research process. Consider the potential for visual learners. Database entries often consist of dense text, overwhelming for some. An AR interface could transform this text into interactive timelines, animated maps, or even short video summaries, making information more accessible and comprehensible. We're talking about translating the abstract data into tangible, experiential learning.

Moreover, this approach significantly improves discoverability. Traditional database searches can feel like navigating a maze, often yielding irrelevant results. With AR integrated into the databases, users could visually explore relevant materials, browsing through thumbnails or 3D representations of articles, images, and even audio recordings. The ability to "preview" resources before committing to a full download is invaluable, particularly in situations with limited bandwidth. This visualization streamlines the research process, facilitating quick access to the most relevant information.

Such integration also opens new avenues for collaborative learning. Imagine students utilizing a shared AR interface during a research session, collaboratively annotating documents, sharing insights, and building a collective understanding of a topic. This shared augmented reality space transcends the limitations of individual workstations, promoting active engagement and collaborative knowledge construction.

The technical implementation, however, necessitates careful planning. Libraries must consider the compatibility of their databases with AR software, ensuring seamless data transfer and user-friendly interface design. This might involve investment in new software, training for librarians, and even potentially the creation of custom AR applications tailored to the specific needs of the library's collections.

Addressing potential challenges is equally crucial. Concerns surrounding data privacy and security must be carefully considered. Implementation requires robust protocols to protect user information while also ensuring the integrity and security of the library's databases. Regular updates and security audits are vital to maintaining a secure environment for users and the library's valuable data assets.

Accessibility for all users is another paramount concern. The AR experience needs to be inclusive, accommodating individuals with visual or other impairments. This means ensuring compatibility with assistive technologies and providing alternative means of accessing information for users who may not be able to utilize the AR interface effectively. This commitment to inclusivity ensures the technology benefits everyone.

The payoff, however, promises a revolutionary transformation. Imagine students immersed in research, experiencing history, literature, or science in entirely new ways. Libraries, no longer passive repositories of information, become dynamic, interactive centers of learning and discovery. The seamless integration of AR with library databases offers a new paradigm in information retrieval and research, enhancing user experience, promoting deeper understanding, and ultimately, fostering a love of learning. It's a leap beyond simply finding information; it's about experiencing it.

3.5 Accessibility and Inclusivity with AR

Augmented reality offers a powerful tool for bridging accessibility gaps within libraries. Consider, for instance, visually impaired patrons.

Standard library catalogs can be challenging to navigate; however, AR applications can provide audio descriptions of book covers, summaries read aloud, and even tactile representations through haptic feedback devices. This technology transcends mere text-based information, offering a multi-sensory experience that greatly enhances accessibility for visually impaired individuals, thus fostering a more inclusive and equitable library environment. Imagine the potential: a world where everyone can fully engage with the vast resources within a library, regardless of their visual capabilities.

For users with motor impairments, AR can similarly be transformative. Instead of physically manipulating books or navigating complex digital interfaces, AR interfaces can be controlled via voice commands or adaptive input devices. Menus can be simplified, text sizes adjusted with ease, and navigation made intuitive through gesture-based controls. This personalized interaction empowers individuals with limited mobility, enabling them to access and utilize library resources independently and with greater ease and efficiency. The focus shifts from physical limitations to engaging content, promoting greater inclusivity and self-reliance.

Furthermore, AR's potential extends beyond visual and motor impairments. For users with cognitive differences, AR applications can offer customizable learning experiences. Information can be presented in simplified formats, with clear visual aids and interactive elements to reinforce comprehension. AR can tailor the experience to individual needs, breaking down complex information into manageable chunks and promoting deeper understanding. Imagine a user with dyslexia benefiting from color-coded text, larger font sizes, or even animated explanations – creating a truly personalized learning environment within the library itself. This is not just about making information available, but about ensuring that every user can fully understand and engage with it.

The integration of AR must be carefully considered to achieve true inclusivity. It is imperative that developers prioritize universal design principles, ensuring that AR applications are usable by people of all abilities. This includes employing intuitive and flexible interfaces, providing multiple input methods, offering clear and concise instructions, and ensuring compatibility with various assistive technologies. Collaboration with disability advocacy groups and user testing with diverse groups is crucial for developing effective and truly inclusive AR applications. This collaborative approach ensures that the technology benefits the broadest possible range of library patrons. Moreover, continuous feedback mechanisms are essential to identify and resolve accessibility issues as they arise and to keep up with advancing technology and evolving needs.

Beyond the technological aspects, promoting inclusivity through AR requires cultural sensitivity and awareness. Language support for multilingual users, culturally relevant content, and consideration of diverse learning styles are all key to creating a welcoming and inclusive environment for all. Simply translating text is insufficient; instead, a deeper understanding of cultural nuances and learning preferences must inform the development of these augmented reality tools. This sensitive and multi-faceted approach, going beyond simple usability, ensures that AR truly empowers all users and reflects the library's commitment to inclusivity and diversity. The aim is not only to make information accessible, but to create a space where everyone feels welcome and valued, regardless of background or abilities. Moreover, libraries should provide training and support for staff on how to use and assist patrons with AR technologies.

4 Virtual Reference Services

Imagine a librarian, not confined to a desk, but present in a virtual space alongside a patron, guiding them through a complex research query. This isn't science fiction; it's the potential of virtual reference services powered by VR and AR. This chapter explores how these technologies can transform the traditional reference interaction, making it more accessible, engaging, and effective.

The limitations of traditional reference services are well-documented. Geographical distance, limited library hours, and the inherent challenges of explaining complex research strategies via phone or email present significant obstacles. VR and AR offer solutions by creating an immersive, interactive environment that transcends these limitations. A librarian can guide a remote user through an online database, virtually pointing to relevant articles and highlighting key information, providing a level of personalized assistance currently unattainable.

Consider the possibilities: a student struggling with a research paper can receive real-time guidance from a librarian in a shared virtual space. The librarian can annotate a digital text together with the student, clarifying concepts and offering alternative search strategies. This shared experience fosters a deeper understanding and creates a more effective learning environment. This is far beyond the limitations of a simple email exchange.

Implementing such a system requires careful planning and training. Librarians need to be equipped with the technical skills and pedagogical expertise to effectively utilize VR and AR technologies. This involves training on the specific software and hardware, but also on how to adapt their teaching and communication styles to this new virtual environment. The goal is not simply to replicate existing reference services digitally, but to leverage the unique capabilities of VR and AR to create a superior experience.

For example, librarians can use VR to conduct virtual library tours, familiarizing patrons with the library's resources and services. This can be particularly useful for new users or those unfamiliar with the library's online catalog. Imagine a virtual tour that guides users through the different sections of the digital library, pointing out key features and providing brief explanations. The possibilities are remarkable, moving beyond the limitations of static online tutorials.

Furthermore, AR applications can enhance the reference experience by overlaying digital information onto physical materials. A librarian can use AR to highlight specific passages in a book during a virtual consultation or show the user related articles from a database in context. This interactive approach can increase understanding and engagement considerably, encouraging deeper interaction with the material. This level of personalized instruction is transformative.

However, successful implementation is dependent on several key factors. Accessibility is paramount. The technology should be user-friendly and adaptable to users with different levels of technological literacy. Librarians need training not only in using the technology itself but also in adapting their teaching methods to this innovative platform. They must become facilitators within this new interactive space.

Training programs should focus on practical application, incorporating real-world scenarios and simulated interactions. Librarians need to develop proficiency in using the tools and understanding how to best leverage their unique capabilities to enhance the reference experience. The focus should be on effective communication and collaboration within the virtual environment. This requires a shift in perspective, transitioning from traditional methods to a more collaborative, dynamic approach to knowledge dissemination.

Another crucial element is the careful selection of appropriate hardware and software. The technology must be reliable, cost-effective, and compatible with the library's existing infrastructure. Choosing the correct platforms will ensure smooth operations and a positive user experience, avoiding potential technical frustrations that could hinder the adoption of the system. The ideal setup must balance affordability with effectiveness and ease of use for both librarians and patrons.

The effective integration of VR/AR into reference services requires a holistic approach, encompassing not only technical training but also pedagogical considerations. Librarians must understand how to adapt their communication styles and teaching methods to the virtual environment, ensuring that the experience is engaging, informative, and supportive. It is about re-imagining the librarian's role within a radically new environment.

Finally, continuous evaluation and improvement are essential. Collecting feedback from both librarians and patrons will help identify areas for improvement and refine the virtual reference service. This iterative process is crucial for ensuring the system remains effective, relevant, and adapts to the evolving needs of users. Continuous improvement means a constantly enhancing and adapting service, meeting the demands of a changing world. The future of reference services is dynamic, adaptive and profoundly changed by the use of immersive technology.

4.1 Remote Assistance via VR/AR

Remote assistance using VR/AR offers a transformative approach to traditional library reference services. Imagine a patron struggling with a complex research query, geographically distant from the library's physical location. Instead of relying solely on email or phone calls, which often lack the visual clarity needed for effective guidance, VR/AR allows for a richer, more intuitive interaction. The librarian can virtually "join" the patron in their space, offering real-time assistance and guidance within the context of the patron's immediate environment. This interactive experience removes the barriers of physical distance, fostering a more personalized and effective learning environment.

This approach leverages the immersive capabilities of VR, allowing the librarian to create a shared virtual space with the patron. This space could be a virtual replica of the library itself, providing a familiar environment for navigating resources, or a customized space tailored to the patron's specific research needs. Using collaborative tools built into the VR environment, the librarian can highlight relevant materials, annotate documents, or even demonstrate specific research techniques directly within the shared virtual environment, thereby dramatically improving the learning process.

Augmented reality, on the other hand, provides a powerful tool for overlaying digital information onto the patron's physical surroundings. Imagine a scenario where a patron needs assistance identifying a specific book on a shelf. Using AR, the librarian can remotely guide the patron by virtually highlighting the book's location on a live video feed from the patron's device. Furthermore, annotations, summaries, and related resources could be overlaid onto the book itself, providing immediate context and enriching the research experience. This seamless blend of physical and digital environments empowers the patron to independently discover and understand information more effectively.

The implementation of such a system requires careful planning and execution. Firstly, librarians need comprehensive training on both the technical aspects of VR/AR technologies and the pedagogical approaches necessary for effective remote instruction within these virtual spaces. This training should encompass not only the use of the technology but also effective communication strategies tailored to the virtual environment. Consider the importance of clear, concise instructions and the effective use of virtual gestures and pointers to maintain clarity in the remote interaction. Accessibility must also be paramount; the system must be compatible with a range of devices and technologies to accommodate patrons with diverse needs and technical capabilities.

Beyond training, robust technical infrastructure is crucial. High-speed internet access for both the librarian and the patron is essential to ensure smooth, lag-free communication within the virtual space. The VR/AR platform should be user-friendly and intuitive, requiring minimal technical expertise from both parties. Regular maintenance and updates are vital to ensure the system's continued functionality and security, including regular testing to anticipate and resolve potential technical glitches. Finally, consider the privacy and security implications of such a system. Data protection protocols must be in place to safeguard sensitive user information and ensure a secure and trustworthy virtual interaction.

The benefits extend beyond simple remote assistance. VR/AR can be used to create immersive virtual workshops or tutorials, allowing librarians to reach a wider audience and provide personalized digital literacy training tailored to the needs of individual patrons. It also offers opportunities for librarians to conduct virtual book talks or author events, expanding the reach of the library's programs and enriching the community engagement opportunities. The system can be integrated with existing library systems, providing a unified and seamless experience for the patron, facilitating efficient management of resources and enhancing the overall library experience.

Ultimately, the successful integration of VR/AR into library reference services hinges on a comprehensive approach that considers the technical aspects, the human factor, and the broader ethical implications. By carefully planning and addressing these crucial elements, libraries can fully harness the power of these technologies to transform remote assistance, enriching the library experience for all and dramatically expanding the reach of library services. The future of reference service lies in this convergence of technology and human connection, bridging geographical barriers and empowering users with intuitive, personalized access to information and expertise. It's a journey that requires investment in training, infrastructure, and careful consideration of the ethical implications, but the potential rewards – a more connected, accessible, and engaging library experience for all – are well worth the effort. The integration of these technologies is not simply about adopting new tools; it's about reinventing the very essence of what it means to provide reference services.

4.2 Training and Education for Librarians

Successful integration of VR/AR into library services hinges on well-trained staff. Librarians need comprehensive training to effectively utilize these technologies and deliver enhanced services. This necessitates a multi-faceted approach, combining theoretical understanding with hands-on practical experience. Initial training should cover the foundational aspects of VR and AR, exploring their differences, functionalities, and potential applications within a library context. This understanding is crucial for librarians to grasp the possibilities and limitations of each technology.

A strong theoretical foundation allows librarians to thoughtfully consider the integration of VR/AR into existing workflows. This goes beyond simply learning how to operate the technology. It's about understanding how to effectively leverage these tools to improve user experiences, enhance research capabilities, and ultimately, better serve the library's community. For example, understanding user interface (UI) and user experience (UX) principles is critical for designing intuitive and accessible virtual library tours or AR-based research tools. Librarians need to be comfortable assessing the usability and accessibility of these technologies, ensuring they meet the needs of all users regardless of their technological proficiency or disabilities. Therefore, an understanding of inclusive design principles becomes paramount.

Practical training is equally crucial, providing librarians with hands-on experience using specific VR/AR tools and platforms relevant to their library's needs. This could involve workshops focusing on 3D modeling software used to create virtual library tours, tutorials on integrating AR with existing library databases, or simulations of virtual reference interactions. These interactive sessions allow librarians to grapple with the challenges of implementing the technology firsthand, troubleshooting potential problems, and becoming proficient in their usage. They provide an opportunity for experimenting with different approaches, adapting strategies based on real-time feedback and improving their overall technical skills. This practical experience enables them to confidently use the technology to provide the best service.

Furthermore, ongoing professional development is essential to stay current with the rapidly evolving VR/AR landscape. This may involve attending conferences, participating in online courses, or engaging in peer-to-peer learning networks. Staying updated on best practices, new software releases, and emerging trends helps librarians maintain proficiency and adapt their skills as the technology advances. The library field, as with many other professions, necessitates continuous learning and adaptation, to prevent falling behind the curve and ensure that services offered are state-of-the-art. The rapid development of virtual and augmented reality demands this commitment to ongoing education.

Training should also encompass pedagogical approaches for incorporating VR/AR into educational programs. Librarians play a vital role in facilitating digital literacy, and understanding how best to integrate these technologies into workshops and learning materials is key. This includes understanding the principles of effective virtual and augmented reality learning design, using gamification to enhance engagement, and adapting instructional methods to different learning styles. Gamification of activities isn't simply adding game-like elements for the sake of entertainment; it's about creating learning experiences that are intrinsically motivating. This training would thus provide librarians with the necessary pedagogical knowledge to design engaging and effective learning experiences.

Beyond the technical and pedagogical aspects, the training curriculum should address ethical and practical considerations. Addressing issues like data privacy, accessibility, and intellectual property rights are crucial elements of responsible technology integration. Training should also cover strategies for managing technical problems, troubleshooting common issues, and providing excellent customer service in virtual and augmented reality environments. Creating a seamless user experience requires not just technical proficiency, but also a deep understanding of user needs and expectations in a virtual environment. It's about providing support and guidance to ensure users can fully benefit from the innovative services offered. Preparing librarians for unexpected challenges, like managing technical glitches during a virtual tour or addressing accessibility concerns for users with disabilities, is essential. The training needs to prepare them to handle these situations with grace and efficiency.

Finally, effective training programs should include opportunities for feedback and assessment. Collecting feedback from librarians on the effectiveness of the training and the usability of the technology allows for continuous improvement. Regular assessments, including practical demonstrations and evaluations, help monitor progress and identify areas needing further development. A well-structured training program utilizes various evaluation methods to gauge learning effectiveness, tailoring its approach to ensure participants acquire the necessary skills and confidence in using VR/AR technologies. This iterative approach, encompassing feedback and assessment, ensures the training program adapts to evolving needs, making it robust and continuously improving. This also allows for the ongoing development of best practices for integrating these technologies into library services. The continuous improvement cycle ensures the library is well-equipped to handle the challenges and embrace the opportunities offered by VR/AR technologies.

5 VR/AR for Digital Literacy Programs

Integrating VR/AR into digital literacy workshops offers a unique opportunity to make learning more engaging and effective. Imagine a workshop where participants don headsets and find themselves inside a virtual library, navigating shelves, searching for information, and interacting with virtual librarians – all within a safe and controlled environment. This immersive experience goes far beyond traditional lectures and handouts; it fosters active participation and encourages deeper understanding. The ability to practice real-world scenarios in a virtual space, such as navigating a complex website or evaluating the credibility of online sources, empowers learners with the confidence to tackle these challenges in the real world. Such active learning environments are crucial for developing the crucial 21st-century digital literacy skills needed to thrive in our increasingly digital society.
Gamification significantly enhances the learning experience within VR/AR digital literacy programs. Think interactive quests where learners must solve puzzles to unlock information, or virtual scavenger hunts that require them to locate specific resources within a simulated online environment. This approach taps into our natural competitive spirit and reward system, boosting motivation and making the learning process intrinsically rewarding. By cleverly designing game mechanics, educators can tailor the difficulty level to suit diverse learning styles and abilities, ensuring inclusivity and fostering a positive learning environment for

all. These gamified elements not only make learning fun, but also promote problem-solving skills, critical thinking, and collaborative learning – skills vital for navigating the complexities of the digital world.

Assessing the effectiveness of VR/AR digital literacy programs requires a multi-faceted approach that goes beyond simple satisfaction surveys. While feedback from participants is certainly valuable, a more rigorous evaluation is essential. This involves incorporating pre\item and post-tests to measure improvements in specific digital literacy skills, analyzing participant engagement metrics within the VR/AR environment (such as time spent on tasks and completion rates), and conducting observations of learner behavior during the workshop sessions. Qualitative data, obtained through interviews or focus groups, can offer rich insights into the learning experience and identify areas for improvement. A comprehensive assessment strategy ensures that programs are effective, valuable, and justify the investment in technology and resources. Moreover, utilizing a combination of quantitative and qualitative methods allows a broader, more detailed, and reliable understanding of the program's impact on digital literacy development.

Designing effective VR/AR digital literacy programs demands careful consideration of several key factors. First, the chosen VR/AR technology must be user-friendly and intuitive, minimizing the learning curve for participants who may lack prior experience with these technologies. Second, the content should be relevant and aligned with the learners' needs and existing digital literacy levels, ensuring the curriculum is both challenging and achievable. Third, the learning activities should be well-structured and sequenced to facilitate progressive skill development. Finally, ample opportunities for instructor-led support and peer interaction should be included. This collaborative learning approach helps build confidence and fosters a sense of community, particularly important for adult learners who may feel intimidated by new technologies. By carefully addressing these key elements, we can ensure the success and effectiveness of VR/AR digital literacy initiatives.

One crucial aspect often overlooked is the need for diverse and inclusive content. The digital world isn't homogenous; it reflects the diversity of its users. Therefore, VR/AR digital literacy programs should strive to represent this diversity, avoiding stereotypes and using imagery and scenarios that resonate with a broad range of learners. This includes considerations of cultural sensitivity, linguistic accessibility, and the needs of learners with disabilities. Ensuring that the programs are accessible to everyone, regardless of background or ability, is not just a matter of inclusivity; it's essential for creating truly effective and impactful learning experiences. This broader approach ensures that everyone can fully benefit from these innovative technologies. Moreover, this inclusivity creates a more equitable digital landscape for all.

The development of effective VR/AR digital literacy programs requires collaboration between librarians, educators, and technology specialists. Librarians bring invaluable expertise in information literacy and user needs. Educators provide insights into effective teaching methodologies and curriculum design, while technology specialists ensure the technical feasibility and smooth operation of the VR/AR systems. This collaborative approach is crucial for aligning the technical capabilities of VR/AR with the pedagogical goals of digital literacy education. By working together, these professionals can create robust, impactful, and accessible programs that empower individuals to navigate the digital world with confidence and competence. A collaborative environment fosters innovation and ensures that the end product effectively meets the needs of its users.

Beyond technical skills, digital literacy encompasses crucial critical thinking abilities, including evaluating information sources, understanding biases, and recognizing misinformation. VR/AR environments provide ideal settings to practice these skills in a risk-free environment. Learners can engage in simulated scenarios where they must evaluate the credibility of online news articles, identify misleading advertisements, or analyze the reliability of social media posts. The interactive nature of these simulations enhances engagement and allows for immediate feedback, solidifying understanding and improving critical analysis abilities. These critical thinking skills are fundamental for responsible and effective participation in the digital world. Furthermore, such skills are essential for navigating the ever-evolving digital landscape.

5.1 Integrating VR/AR into Workshops

Designing effective VR/AR workshops requires careful planning. Consider your target audience's tech proficiency; beginners might need more hand-holding than experienced users. Start with the basics, introducing VR headsets and AR applications gently, ensuring everyone feels comfortable before moving to complex interactions. A gradual approach avoids overwhelming participants and encourages active engagement. Remember to create a supportive learning environment where questions are welcomed, and mistakes are viewed as opportunities for learning. This fosters confidence and ensures everyone participates fully. Provide clear, concise instructions, using simple language and avoiding jargon. Demonstrate each step clearly, using both visual aids and verbal explanations. This multi-sensory approach improves comprehension and retention. Pair participants to encourage peer-to-peer learning and problem-solving. Observing others can often highlight subtle techniques or solutions participants might have missed. Regular breaks help prevent fatigue and maintain focus, ensuring participants remain engaged and productive. Consider offering refreshments and a relaxed atmosphere to enhance the learning experience.

Practical exercises are vital for reinforcing learning. Design interactive activities that allow participants to apply newly acquired skills immediately. For example, a VR library tour could allow users to practice navigation within a virtual space. Similarly, AR-based exercises could involve overlaying information onto real-world library resources, facilitating practical application of AR techniques. Provide feedback throughout the exercises, offering constructive criticism and highlighting areas for improvement. This ensures participants are on the right track and allows them to address any difficulties before proceeding. Make the exercises fun and engaging; gamification can significantly boost participation and motivation, making learning a more enjoyable experience for everyone. Consider incorporating elements of competition or collaboration to stimulate interaction and encourage team work.

Assessment is crucial to gauge workshop effectiveness. Implement pre\item and post-workshop quizzes to measure knowledge acquisition and identify areas needing further attention. Use a combination of multiple-choice, short-answer, and practical exercises to evaluate different aspects of learning. Provide constructive feedback on assessments, not just grades, highlighting areas of strength and recommending strategies for improvement. This feedback loop is vital for improving the workshop design and content. Observe participants during exercises, taking notes on their engagement and challenges. These observations provide valuable insights into the effectiveness of different teaching methods. Gather feedback through surveys, allowing participants to share their experiences and suggest improvements. Analyze the gathered data to evaluate the overall impact of the workshop and to inform future iterations.

Successfully integrating VR/AR into workshops demands careful consideration of accessibility. Ensure the hardware and software are compatible with various disabilities. Offer alternative methods for those unable to use standard VR/AR equipment. Provide alternative formats for workshop materials, like transcripts of videos or large-print handouts. Create a welcoming and inclusive environment where all participants feel comfortable contributing. This ensures equitable access to the learning experience. Consider language accessibility; offer multilingual resources and interpreters if necessary. These simple steps ensure everyone can participate meaningfully in the workshop, and benefit from the skills acquired. Adapt exercises to meet different learning styles; cater to visual, auditory, and kinesthetic learners. This ensures that the material resonates with all participants.

Finally, continuously evaluate and improve your workshops. Regularly review participant feedback, assess learning outcomes, and adapt the content based on this feedback loop. Stay updated on the latest advancements in VR/AR technology to incorporate new tools and techniques. Attend relevant conferences and workshops to expand your knowledge and stay current in this rapidly evolving field. This continuous improvement ensures your workshops remain engaging, effective, and up-to-date with the latest technology developments. Remember that the ongoing adaptation of the workshops is just as vital as the initial design. By embracing continuous improvement, you can enhance the learning experience and maximize the effectiveness of your VR/AR workshops, helping librarians and information professionals to effectively leverage cutting-edge technology.

5.2 Gamification and Interactive Learning

Gamification, the application of game-design elements in non-game contexts, offers a powerful tool for enhancing digital literacy programs within the library setting. By incorporating elements like points, badges, leaderboards, and narrative structures, we can transform potentially dry learning experiences into engaging and rewarding activities. Imagine a virtual scavenger hunt across a 3D model of the library, where participants earn points for finding specific books or answering research-related questions. This approach not only increases user engagement but also fosters a sense of accomplishment and healthy competition.

The key to successful gamification lies in thoughtful design. It's not simply about slapping game mechanics onto existing content; rather, it requires a deep understanding of learning objectives and the target audience. For example, a gamified tutorial on database searching could be structured as a quest, with challenges requiring users to locate specific information within different databases. Each successful search could reward the user with points and unlock new challenges, creating a sense of progression and motivating them to learn more. Carefully chosen rewards—virtual badges reflecting their newly acquired skills, access to exclusive online resources, or even a real-world prize—can further amplify the impact.

Interactive learning, closely related to gamification, goes beyond simply adding game elements. It aims to create active learning experiences where users are actively involved in the process of knowledge construction. This could involve collaborative projects within a virtual library space, allowing participants to work together on research tasks or create virtual exhibits showcasing their findings. The interactive nature of these activities fosters critical thinking, problem-solving skills, and collaboration, crucial skills for navigating the information-rich digital

world.
The design of interactive learning experiences in VR/AR requires careful consideration of user interface and user experience (UI/UX) principles. A well-designed interface should be intuitive and easy to navigate, ensuring that users can easily access resources and engage with the learning materials. Moreover, incorporating elements of adaptive learning, where the difficulty level adjusts based on the user's progress, can personalize the experience and cater to individual learning styles. Consider the use of avatars, allowing users to represent themselves within the virtual environment, potentially fostering a more engaging and personalized learning experience.
Implementing gamified and interactive learning modules requires careful planning and execution. First, clearly define the learning objectives and identify the specific skills or knowledge you want participants to acquire. Then, design the game mechanics and interactive elements in a way that directly supports these objectives. For example, a points-based system could reward users for successfully completing specific tasks, while leaderboards could foster friendly competition. It's crucial to ensure that these elements are not merely superficial additions but are integrated thoughtfully into the learning process, ensuring they enhance understanding and skill acquisition rather than distracting from it.
Finally, assess the effectiveness of your gamified and interactive learning programs through various methods. Quantitative data, such as completion rates and scores, can provide insights into the engagement and effectiveness of the program. Qualitative data, such as user feedback and observations, can offer valuable insights into the user experience and identify areas for improvement. By employing a mixed-methods approach to evaluation, librarians can gain a comprehensive understanding of the impact of gamification and interactive learning on participants' knowledge acquisition and skill development. This allows for continuous refinement and improvement, maximizing the effectiveness of your program and ensuring a worthwhile experience for your patrons. The ultimate goal is not just engagement, but demonstrable improvements in digital literacy skills. Remember that regular evaluation and adap-

tation are key to the success of any innovative program.

5.3 Assessing Learning Outcomes

Measuring the success of VR/AR integration in digital literacy programs requires a multifaceted approach, moving beyond simple satisfaction surveys. We need robust methods that truly reflect the learning achieved. For instance, pre\item and post-tests assessing knowledge of specific digital literacy skills, like online safety or information evaluation, provide quantifiable data demonstrating improvement. These tests should be carefully designed, covering a range of complexity levels, to ensure a comprehensive evaluation of the learners' progress. The questions themselves should be diverse, incorporating multiple-choice, short-answer, and even practical application scenarios to gauge different aspects of understanding. Consider including questions that directly relate to specific VR/AR elements of the program to see how effectively those tools facilitated learning.

Beyond formal assessments, we can leverage observational methods. During VR/AR sessions, trained observers can unobtrusively monitor learner engagement and interaction. Noteworthy behaviors could include active participation, problem-solving approaches, and the effective use of VR/AR features. This qualitative data offers valuable insights into how learners interact with the technology and how well they apply their new skills within the virtual environment. The data collected needs rigorous analysis, potentially using coding schemes to categorize observed behaviors for meaningful interpretation and comparison. Remember to establish clear observation protocols beforehand to maintain consistency and reduce bias.

Learner feedback is crucial; however, we need to move beyond simple satisfaction ratings. Instead, use structured interviews or focus groups to understand how effectively the VR/AR elements aided their learning process. Encourage participants to reflect on specific examples where the technology proved helpful or presented challenges. This will reveal practical insights into the strengths and weaknesses of the program design and technology implementation. Consider using open-ended questions that allow participants to articulate their experiences in their own words to gather rich, detailed information. Analyze these responses thematically to identify recurring patterns and overarching insights.

To fully understand the impact of the program, incorporate a longitudinal perspective. Follow-up surveys or interviews conducted several weeks or months after the program's completion can reveal the long-term retention of knowledge and skills. This reveals whether the learning was genuinely impactful or merely temporary, and can help refine future programs. Compare the results of these long-term assessments with the initial pre\item and post-tests to see how knowledge retention is affected over time and to potentially identify factors that influenced this retention rate.

Finally, remember ethical considerations. Maintain participant confidentiality throughout the assessment process. Use anonymized data whenever possible and follow established guidelines for data security and protection. Informed consent is essential; ensure participants understand the purpose of the evaluation and how their data will be used. Transparency and respect for participants are paramount in ensuring a robust and ethical evaluation. Any data analysis should include a robust explanation of the methodology, any potential biases identified, and the limitations of the study. Only then can your assessment fully contribute to the evolution of effective VR/AR-based digital literacy programs.

6 Challenges and Opportunities

High initial investment costs represent a significant hurdle for many libraries, particularly smaller ones with limited budgets. Securing funding through grants, partnerships with technology companies, or fundraising initiatives becomes crucial. Successful implementation necessitates a strategic approach, prioritizing projects with demonstrable impact and aligning them with the library's overall mission. Careful planning and a phased rollout can minimize financial strain and maximize resource utilization, building a foundation for future expansions. Ignoring the financial aspect can quickly lead to unsustainable projects, therefore, meticulous budgeting and long-term planning are essential for successful VR/AR integration.

Accessibility remains a critical concern. Not all users possess the necessary technological literacy or physical capabilities to fully engage with VR/AR experiences. Libraries need to invest in training programs for staff and users alike, ensuring everyone can comfortably navigate the technology. Furthermore, designing inclusive experiences, accounting for diverse learning styles and disabilities, is paramount. Adapting interfaces for users with visual impairments, hearing loss, or motor limitations, through the incorporation of alternative interaction methods and assistive technologies, is an absolute necessity. Failure to address accessibility can result in the exclusion of significant portions of the library's community.

Privacy and data security are paramount. Collecting and storing user data for personalized experiences requires robust security measures. Compliance with relevant privacy regulations and data protection laws is essential, maintaining transparency regarding data usage policies. This needs to be addressed by developing comprehensive data security protocols, implementing encryption, and employing secure data storage practices. Failure to do so could lead to breaches of privacy, damage to the library's reputation, and potential legal repercussions. Building user trust necessitates careful consideration of data protection and the implementation of user-friendly privacy policies.

Despite these challenges, the opportunities are immense. VR/AR technology presents a unique chance to create innovative and engaging library experiences. Imagine virtual tours of historical archives, allowing users to explore collections remotely, or immersive storytelling experiences, bringing historical figures and events to life. The potential to reach wider audiences and enhance engagement with library resources is truly transformative. Moreover, AR can enhance traditional research methods by layering digital information onto physical books, offering a richer learning experience. This integration not only transforms learning but also addresses the needs of a digitally savvy population, thereby enhancing the library's relevance and value.

The integration of VR/AR into library services is not just about technology; it's about enhancing the library's role in the community. By providing accessible, engaging, and innovative experiences, libraries can better serve their users and strengthen their position as vital community hubs. Embracing these technologies allows libraries to remain at the forefront of information access and learning, adapting to the evolving needs of the information age. The strategic implementation of these technologies, with a focus on inclusive design, robust security protocols, and thoughtful user engagement, creates a compelling pathway towards a more vibrant and accessible library experience for all. This necessitates a shift from passive information dissemination to active participation, transforming libraries into interactive learning spaces. Investing in these transformative technologies should be seen not as an expense, but as a crucial investment in the future of libraries and the communities they serve. Failing to embrace this change risks losing the opportunity to remain relevant in an increasingly digital world. Forward-thinking libraries are already integrating VR/AR to foster user engagement, showcasing the transformative potential of these technologies to connect with diverse audiences and offer enriching learning experiences.

The future success of VR/AR integration within libraries hinges on collaboration. Partnership with technology providers, educational institutions, and other community organizations provides access to expertise, resources, and support. Sharing best practices and fostering a collaborative environment accelerates innovation and ensures sustainable implementation across the library sector. By working together, libraries can address the challenges and maximize the opportunities presented by VR/AR, building a future where technology enhances access to information and enriches the lives of library users. The power of collaboration should not be underestimated. Creating a collaborative environment facilitates the sharing of expertise, resources, and knowledge leading to enhanced problem-solving, quicker implementation and overall increased success of VR/AR integration in libraries.

6.1 Technological Barriers and Costs

The initial hurdle for many libraries considering VR/AR integration is the substantial upfront cost. High-quality VR headsets, AR devices, and the software needed to create immersive experiences represent a significant financial investment, often exceeding the budgets of smaller libraries or those lacking dedicated technology funding. This includes not only the hardware itself but also the licensing fees for specialized software, potentially requiring substantial ongoing maintenance and software updates. Moreover, the need for powerful computers and potentially dedicated servers to render complex 3D environments adds further expense. Successfully implementing VR/AR demands careful budgeting and a comprehensive cost-benefit analysis, identifying potential funding sources and justifying the expense based on anticipated improvements in library services and user engagement.

Beyond the immediate purchase price, ongoing operational costs must also be considered. This includes technical support, software updates, maintenance of hardware, and potential staff training. Maintaining the equipment requires specialized knowledge and may necessitate contracting with external IT support, adding to the overall expense. The lifespan of VR/AR technology is shorter than that of traditional library resources, necessitating frequent upgrades to keep pace with technological advancements and maintain a high level of user experience. Libraries need to anticipate these recurrent costs and build them into their long-term budgetary planning.

Technical expertise is another significant barrier. Implementing and maintaining VR/AR systems demands specialized technical skills that many libraries may lack. Creating immersive 3D environments, developing interactive interfaces, and troubleshooting technical glitches require experienced professionals with expertise in 3D modeling, software development, and network administration. Hiring or training personnel with these skills adds to the overall cost and may necessitate outsourcing certain tasks, increasing financial burdens. Without adequate technical support, the library risks system malfunctions, poor user experience, and ultimately, the failure of the VR/AR initiative.

Compatibility issues across different devices and platforms also pose a challenge. The VR/AR landscape is constantly evolving, with various headsets, software, and platforms emerging regularly. Ensuring compatibility across different devices and platforms requires careful planning and selection of compatible technologies. Libraries must also consider the needs of their diverse users, some of whom may have limited access to compatible devices or possess different levels of technological proficiency. Addressing compatibility issues requires ongoing attention to technological advancements and strategic choices that balance affordability, user experience, and long-term maintenance.

Finally, the digital divide presents a significant barrier to equitable access. While VR/AR promises to enhance library services, its implementation could inadvertently exacerbate existing inequalities in access to technology. Not all library patrons will own VR/AR devices or have the necessary technological literacy to use them effectively. Libraries must therefore consider strategies to ensure equitable access, potentially providing on-site VR/AR experiences, offering workshops and training sessions to equip patrons with the necessary skills, or collaborating with community organizations to broaden access to technology. Addressing the digital divide requires proactive planning and a commitment to inclusivity to ensure that the benefits of VR/AR are shared by all library users. Overcoming these barriers requires a holistic approach, combining strategic planning, robust budgeting, and a commitment to providing equitable access to all members of the community.

6.2 Accessibility and Inclusivity

Creating accessible and inclusive virtual and augmented reality experiences within libraries requires careful consideration of diverse user needs. We must move beyond simply adding technology; instead, we must design with accessibility at the core of our development process. This means actively involving people with disabilities in the design and testing phases. Their feedback is invaluable in identifying and rectifying accessibility barriers before they become ingrained in the final product. Ignoring this crucial step risks creating technology that excludes the very individuals we aim to serve, thereby undermining the intended benefits of VR/AR integration.

Designing for diverse users necessitates understanding the wide spectrum of disabilities. Visual impairments require careful consideration of alternative input methods, such as voice commands and haptic feedback, rather than relying solely on visual cues. Auditory impairments demand clear visual instructions and appropriate text-to-speech functionality. Motor impairments need intuitive and adaptable interfaces supporting various input devices, including joysticks, eye-tracking systems, and adaptive switches. Cognitive impairments require simplified navigation, clear and concise instructions, and the option for adjustable levels of complexity to accommodate varying cognitive abilities.

Moreover, linguistic diversity is another key aspect of inclusivity. Our virtual library experiences must accommodate users who speak various languages. This can be achieved through multilingual support within the interface, offering translations of key instructions and information.

Subtitles and closed captions for audio elements are essential, ensuring access for users with hearing difficulties and those in different linguistic backgrounds. Employing culturally sensitive design principles further enhances inclusivity by ensuring the virtual environments and their content resonate with a diverse range of users and do not perpetuate biases.

Technological accessibility involves more than just adapting interfaces. We must also consider the technical accessibility of the hardware itself. Many VR headsets and AR devices might not be compatible with assistive technologies. This calls for researching and prioritizing technologies that are inherently accessible or have strong adaptive capabilities. Collaboration with assistive technology providers is vital in integrating our VR/AR systems seamlessly with existing user support structures. The use of open standards for development is strongly recommended to ensure maximum compatibility and interoperability with assistive tools.

Financial accessibility represents another critical hurdle. The cost of VR/AR equipment can be prohibitive for many users. Libraries should explore partnerships with technology providers to secure affordable access to equipment for patrons with limited financial resources. Exploring options such as loaner programs, communal spaces, and community outreach initiatives can contribute to bridging this financial divide. Public awareness campaigns can also highlight the benefits of VR/AR technology for all users, fostering a greater understanding of its value for people with disabilities.

Beyond technical accessibility, we must focus on usability. A user-friendly interface that is intuitive and easy to navigate is crucial for everyone, especially people with disabilities. This includes clear visual hierarchy, appropriate font sizes and styles, and consistent labeling of interactive elements. Testing our interfaces with diverse groups, including users with various disabilities, is paramount to uncovering usability issues and making improvements. Incorporating user feedback from the testing stage is vital in refining our design, creating a more inclusive and welcoming environment for everyone.

Finally, we must ensure that our VR/AR library experiences are not only accessible but also engaging. A truly inclusive system is not just about providing access; it's about offering a positive and enriching experience for all users. This requires creative use of design principles that cater to diverse learning styles and preferences. By integrating diverse content, perspectives, and interactive elements, we can develop systems that are not only accessible but also inspiring and enriching. Only through this combined approach of inclusive design, proactive testing, and user-centered development can we create VR/AR environments in libraries that genuinely serve all members of our communities.

6.3 Privacy and Security Concerns

Data security is paramount. Think of the sensitive patron information handled daily—addresses, phone numbers, borrowing history, even potentially sensitive research topics. A breach could have severe consequences, damaging trust and potentially exposing users to identity theft or other serious harms. Robust cybersecurity measures, including strong encryption, access control systems, and regular security audits, are non-negotiable. Failure to implement these safeguards could lead to legal liabilities and irreparable reputational damage. Consider the potential for data loss; a single point of failure in the system could wipe out years' worth of collected data. Regular backups and disaster recovery planning are not optional additions; they are essential components of a comprehensive security plan. Furthermore, keeping software updated and regularly patching vulnerabilities are also crucial, as outdated systems are easy targets for malicious actors.

Privacy concerns are equally significant. The use of VR and AR technologies often involves collecting user data, including location information, usage patterns, and even biometric data in some advanced applications. This data collection must be transparent and ethically sound. Users need to understand exactly what information is being collected, why it's being collected, how it will be used, and how it will be protected. Clear, concise, and easily understandable privacy policies are essential, avoiding legal jargon and technical terms. Moreover, obtaining informed consent is vital. Users should have control over their data and the ability to opt out of data collection if they choose. Providing clear mechanisms for data access, correction, and deletion allows users to maintain control over their personal information. Ignoring these critical privacy considerations risks alienating patrons and jeopardizing the library's reputation.

The potential for misuse of these technologies is another factor to consider carefully. VR and AR experiences can be manipulated or exploited for malicious purposes, including creating immersive environments for phishing scams or spreading misinformation. Librarians must be trained to identify and mitigate these risks, and the systems themselves should be designed with security in mind. Robust authentication and authorization protocols are necessary to prevent unauthorized access. Monitoring user activity can help detect suspicious behavior, but this must be done ethically and transparently, without compromising user privacy. Regular security assessments by independent experts are an invaluable step to uncover and address potential vulnerabilities that might be missed by internal teams. Remember, proactive measures are far more effective and less expensive than reactive damage control following a security breach.

Beyond technological solutions, effective communication is crucial. Librarians must be able to explain the security and privacy measures in place to patrons, building trust and assuring them that their information is safe. Open communication fosters transparency and accountability, demonstrating a commitment to user privacy and data protection. Furthermore, clear guidelines and policies are necessary to define acceptable use of VR/AR technologies within the library context, preventing misuse and establishing expectations for user behavior. Regular staff training on these policies and procedures is essential. It's not simply enough to have strong security measures in place; the library must also proactively educate its users about online safety and responsible technology use. This includes teaching patrons how to spot and avoid phishing attempts and misinformation, ensuring they can navigate the digital world with confidence and awareness. Developing a culture of security awareness within the library is a continuous process, not a one-time event.

Finally, remember that technology is constantly evolving, and so are the associated risks. Staying updated with the latest security threats and best practices is an ongoing commitment. Continuous improvement is key. Regular reviews of security protocols and privacy policies are essential to adapt to the changing landscape of cyber threats. Collaboration with other institutions and cybersecurity experts allows for the sharing of best practices and the collective addressing of evolving challenges. By fostering a culture of security awareness and staying abreast of emerging threats, libraries can confidently integrate VR/AR technologies while safeguarding user privacy and data security. This is more than simply following guidelines; it's a commitment to building a trusted and secure environment for all library users. The integration of these powerful technologies should be guided by a strong ethical compass and a steadfast commitment to safeguarding user data.

7 Future Trends and Conclusion

The integration of VR/AR in libraries is poised for exponential growth. Imagine a future where accessing rare manuscripts involves a seamless VR journey to a distant archive, or where students explore ancient civilizations through immersive AR overlays on textbooks. This isn't science fiction; it's the rapidly approaching reality shaped by advancements in affordable hardware, intuitive software, and increasingly sophisticated content creation tools. The Metaverse, a persistent shared virtual world, represents a particularly exciting frontier. Libraries can establish dedicated Metaverse spaces, offering virtual branches, interactive exhibits, and collaborative learning environments accessible globally, transcending geographical limitations and democratizing access to information like never before.

This evolution necessitates a proactive approach to skill development. Librarians will need specialized training in VR/AR technologies, 3D modeling, user experience design, and digital content creation. Furthermore, a shift in traditional roles is inevitable; librarians will become curators and facilitators of immersive experiences, guiding users through virtual spaces and leveraging these technologies to enhance traditional services. Collaboration with technology experts and educational institutions is crucial to ensure libraries have the resources and personnel to successfully navigate this transformation. The ongoing evolution of VR/AR itself also presents both opportunities and challenges. We'll see advancements in haptic feedback, higher-resolution displays, and more sophisticated AI-driven interaction design which will lead to richer, more engaging and intuitive library experiences.

However, ethical considerations must remain central to the adoption of these technologies. Privacy concerns related to user data within virtual environments require careful attention. We need robust data protection policies and transparent communication with users regarding data collection and usage. Equitable access is another critical ethical concern. Libraries must proactively ensure VR/AR services are accessible to all users, irrespective of socioeconomic background, physical ability, or digital literacy. This might involve providing accessible hardware and software, creating inclusive virtual spaces, and offering training programs to bridge the digital divide. Consideration must also be given to the potential for bias embedded within VR/AR applications, ensuring fair and unbiased access to information and resources for all users.

The next steps for libraries involve strategic planning, resource allocation, and staff training. Libraries will need to identify specific areas where VR/AR can best serve their users' needs, setting clear goals and evaluating the return on investment for technology acquisitions. This strategic approach should prioritize user needs and ensure that technology enhances, rather than supplants, core library services. Continuous evaluation of VR/AR initiatives is essential to identify areas for improvement and to ensure that these technologies remain relevant and effective. This involves gathering user feedback, analyzing usage data, and adapting services to meet evolving needs. Open communication and collaboration within the library community are also essential to share best practices, lessons learned, and resources that will help to accelerate the adoption and successful implementation of VR/AR technologies across all library systems.

In conclusion, the future of libraries is intertwined with the advancement of VR/AR. By embracing these technologies responsibly and proactively addressing the accompanying challenges, libraries can position themselves to provide enhanced services, reach wider audiences, and redefine their role in the information ecosystem of tomorrow. This is not merely about adding a new tool to the existing toolkit; it's about fundamentally reshaping the way people engage with information and knowledge, thereby fulfilling the library's enduring mission of providing access to all. The journey will require careful navigation, but the potential rewards – increased engagement, expanded access, and a richer learning experience for all – are immense and well worth the effort. The proactive adoption of these technologies ensures libraries remain at the forefront of information access and dissemination, securing their place as vital community hubs in the digital age and beyond. The challenge, and the opportunity, is to shape this future thoughtfully and ethically, ensuring that technology empowers rather than limits accessibility and inclusivity.

7.1 The Metaverse and Libraries

The Metaverse presents a unique opportunity for libraries to transcend physical limitations and reach a global audience. Imagine a virtual library branch existing alongside its physical counterpart, accessible 24/7 from anywhere with an internet connection. This isn't science fiction; it's a realistic potential application of the Metaverse's immersive capabilities. Users could explore virtual shelves, interact with digital artifacts, and attend virtual events, all within a richly textured and engaging environment. The potential for collaborative research and knowledge sharing within such a space is immense.

Consider the implications for accessibility. Individuals with physical limitations, geographical constraints, or disabilities could readily participate in library programs and access resources previously unavailable to them. The Metaverse offers an inclusive environment that removes many of the traditional barriers to library services. This virtual access could transform how libraries serve marginalized communities and individuals with limited mobility.

However, the integration of libraries into the Metaverse isn't without its challenges. Creating and maintaining these digital spaces demands significant technological expertise and financial investment. Libraries will need to develop new skills in areas such as 3D modeling, virtual environment design, and user interface development. Collaboration with technology experts and the exploration of innovative funding models will be crucial for successful implementation.

Moreover, the issue of digital literacy cannot be overlooked. Providing training and support to both staff and patrons will be essential for ensuring effective navigation and engagement within the virtual library space. This means libraries need to incorporate digital literacy training programs to equip their communities with the skills they will need to participate fully within the Metaverse. These programs should focus not just on basic computer skills, but also on understanding and navigating virtual environments, interacting with digital objects, and utilizing the unique features offered by the Metaverse.

Security and privacy concerns are paramount. Protecting user data and ensuring the safety of virtual spaces will be essential for maintaining trust and building confidence within this new environment. Libraries will need to adopt robust security protocols to safeguard user information and mitigate the risks associated with operating in a digital realm. This includes implementing appropriate data encryption, access controls, and privacy policies consistent with existing library regulations and best practices.

The success of Metaverse integration also hinges on carefully considering the user experience. The virtual library must be intuitive, engaging, and easy to navigate for users of all ages and technical skill levels. This necessitates prioritizing user-centered design principles throughout the development and implementation process. Libraries must actively seek user feedback to ensure their Metaverse presence is effective and caters to the diverse needs of their communities.

The potential benefits, however, far outweigh the challenges. The Metaverse offers libraries an unparalleled opportunity to expand their reach, enhance their services, and engage with their communities in innovative ways. By embracing this emerging technology, libraries can reinforce their position as vital centers for learning, information access, and community engagement in the digital age. This strategic integration will require proactive planning, investment in technology and staff training, and a commitment to addressing the ethical and practical concerns of operating within this new landscape. The future of libraries might well be interwoven with the fabric of the Metaverse, offering a richer, more accessible, and more inclusive experience for all. The journey requires careful planning and collaboration, but the potential rewards for libraries and their communities are immense.

7.2 Emerging Technologies and their Impact

The integration of emerging technologies beyond VR and AR presents both exciting opportunities and significant challenges for libraries. Consider the potential of blockchain technology, for instance. Secure, transparent record-keeping of library materials, provenance tracking for historical documents, and even decentralized access control systems are all possibilities. The implications for managing digital collections and ensuring intellectual property rights are profound. Implementing such a system would require careful consideration of security protocols and user privacy, a challenge that many libraries currently face. However, the payoff could be substantial, providing increased security and trust in library data. This could also enhance the library's role as a trusted source of information in the increasingly complex digital landscape.

Artificial intelligence, specifically machine learning algorithms, offers another transformative potential. Beyond basic search function improvements, AI could power advanced recommendation systems, anticipating user needs and suggesting relevant resources proactively. Imagine a system that can analyze a user's research history and suggest related materials even before they begin their search, significantly enhancing the research process. This would, however, necessitate considerable investment in infrastructure and ongoing maintenance, and ethical considerations surrounding data privacy must be central to the implementation strategy. Furthermore, the potential for bias within AI algorithms needs careful scrutiny and mitigation to ensure equitable access to information.

The Internet of Things (IoT) presents yet another avenue for innovation. Smart sensors could monitor environmental conditions within the library, optimizing energy consumption and preserving valuable collections. Imagine real-time alerts for temperature fluctuations or humidity spikes, enabling proactive intervention and preventing potential damage. IoT-enabled access control and asset tracking could also improve library security and efficiency, offering detailed information on usage patterns and resource allocation. However, the integration of IoT devices raises concerns regarding data security and potential vulnerabilities to cyberattacks, requiring robust security measures to protect sensitive information.

Furthermore, the development of advanced haptic technologies could revolutionize the way users interact with digital library resources. Imagine a user being able to 'feel' the texture of a historical manuscript through a haptic glove while exploring a virtual exhibit, or experiencing the tactile sensations of turning the pages of a rare book in a VR environment. This level of sensory immersion could greatly enhance user engagement and understanding. However, the technological maturity and cost of these technologies remain a hurdle to immediate implementation.

Finally, the rise of 5G and beyond networks promises to significantly impact the user experience. Faster download speeds and lower latency will be crucial for supporting immersive VR/AR applications and streaming high-resolution digital content. The accessibility of cloud-based services will increase, allowing libraries to offer a broader range of virtual and augmented reality resources. Yet, reliable, high-speed internet access is not ubiquitous. Addressing the digital divide remains paramount to ensuring equal access to the benefits of these emerging technologies. This creates a need for innovative strategies and collaborative efforts to bridge the gap between those with access and those without. Digital literacy programs, a key focus of this book, become even more crucial in this context. The future success of integrating these technologies depends on our ability to navigate this complexity successfully and inclusively.

7.3 The Future of Library Services

The integration of virtual and augmented reality isn't merely a technological upgrade; it's a fundamental shift in how we conceive of and interact with information. Libraries, traditionally seen as repositories of physical books, are evolving into dynamic, immersive learning environments. This transformation is fueled by the potential of VR/AR to provide personalized, engaging, and accessible experiences, surpassing the limitations of traditional library services.

Imagine a world where students can virtually explore ancient libraries like Alexandria, interacting with digitized texts and artifacts, all from the comfort of their local branch. This isn't science fiction; it's the promise of VR technology bringing historical contexts to life, fostering a deeper appreciation for learning. This level of engagement far exceeds the static display of a textbook or a museum exhibit.

Consider the possibilities for remote users. Individuals in rural areas, or those with mobility challenges, can now access the same rich resources as urban dwellers. Virtual reference librarians can provide personalized assistance, guiding users through digital collections and answering complex research questions in real-time, regardless of geographical location. This creates a truly equitable and inclusive access to knowledge.

Augmented reality offers a different, yet equally transformative, approach. Imagine a student using an AR app to overlay historical context onto a physical book. A tap on a paragraph might reveal a 3D model of a Roman chariot, or a video interview with a prominent historian. This technology bridges the gap between the physical and the digital, enriching the learning experience in ways that were previously unimaginable.

The implications for digital literacy are substantial. VR/AR can make learning fun and engaging, particularly for younger generations who are already comfortable with immersive technologies. Interactive games and simulations can teach valuable skills, while virtual workshops can cater to diverse learning styles and preferences.

However, the path towards this future isn't without its challenges. The initial investment in hardware and software can be substantial. Equitable access for all users requires careful consideration of digital divides and the need for accessible interfaces. Privacy and security are crucial considerations, especially when handling sensitive user data.

Overcoming these hurdles requires proactive measures. Libraries need to collaborate with technology providers, educators, and policymakers to develop affordable, accessible, and secure VR/AR solutions. Investing in staff training is vital to ensure librarians can effectively utilize and maintain these technologies. Community engagement and careful planning are crucial to build support and address potential concerns.

Libraries of the future will be more than just places to borrow books; they will be dynamic centers of learning and discovery, leveraging the power of VR/AR to connect people with information in unprecedented ways. This requires a forward-thinking approach, embracing innovation while carefully addressing the ethical and logistical challenges involved. The reward, however, is a more inclusive, engaging, and effective library experience for all. It's about not just preserving the past, but shaping the future of learning. It's about making knowledge accessible and exciting for everyone, regardless of their circumstances. And that is the true potential of VR/AR in libraries—a future where learning is limitless, engaging, and accessible to all.

7.4 Ethical Considerations

The integration of VR/AR into library services presents a unique ethical landscape demanding careful consideration. Data privacy, a paramount concern, requires robust security measures to protect user information collected through these technologies. This includes clear and transparent privacy policies, informing users about data collection practices, and implementing strong encryption protocols to safeguard sensitive data. Failure to address this could lead to breaches of trust and potential legal ramifications. Furthermore, the potential for bias embedded within VR/AR applications must be acknowledged and actively mitigated. Algorithmic bias, for instance, could unfairly influence search results or resource recommendations, leading to inequitable access to information.

Rigorous testing and auditing are crucial to identify and address such biases, ensuring fairness and equitable access for all library patrons.

Maintaining accessibility for all users is another critical ethical imperative. The immersive nature of VR/AR, while innovative, presents challenges for users with disabilities. Designers and librarians must prioritize inclusivity by ensuring compatibility with assistive technologies and developing user interfaces that cater to diverse needs and abilities. This includes providing alternative methods of interaction for users with visual, auditory, or motor impairments. Failing to address this aspect undermines the library's commitment to serving all members of its community.

The potential for misuse of VR/AR technologies also necessitates careful ethical planning. The creation of realistic virtual environments could lead to the spread of misinformation or the perpetuation of harmful stereotypes. Libraries must establish guidelines and implement content filtering mechanisms to prevent the dissemination of inaccurate or offensive material. Promoting media literacy among users is equally important, empowering them to critically evaluate the information encountered in virtual and augmented environments.

Furthermore, the equitable distribution of resources and opportunities associated with VR/AR technologies warrants attention. The cost of implementation and maintenance can be substantial, potentially creating disparities between resource-rich and under-resourced libraries. Strategies to address this imbalance are necessary, including collaborative initiatives, funding programs, and open-source software development to promote widespread accessibility. Ensuring that these technologies do not exacerbate existing inequalities is crucial to upholding the library's role as a vital community resource.

Beyond these immediate concerns, the longer-term ethical implications of VR/AR in libraries warrant ongoing reflection. As these technologies evolve, their potential impact on user behavior, social interaction, and cognitive development requires continuous monitoring and evaluation. Regular ethical reviews, involving librarians, technology specialists, and community members, are essential to guide responsible innovation and ensure that these transformative technologies serve the best interests of the library and its patrons. Proactive engagement with these complex ethical considerations will be crucial for navigating this evolving landscape and harnessing the full potential of VR/AR while upholding the core values of the library. The goal is not merely to embrace new technologies, but to do so in a manner that strengthens the library's commitment to equity, accessibility, and the responsible dissemination of information. This requires ongoing dialogue, collaboration, and a commitment to adapting ethical frameworks as the technology advances. A proactive and thoughtful approach is essential to ensuring that VR/AR enhances, rather than undermines, the library's vital role in society. The responsible implementation of these technologies necessitates a deep understanding of ethical principles and a willingness to adapt to the unique challenges they present. The ethical considerations are not static; they evolve alongside the technology itself, requiring continuous reflection and adaptation. This ongoing ethical assessment will be critical to ensure that virtual and augmented reality serve as powerful tools for advancing the mission of libraries and strengthening their position as vital community anchors.

7.5 Next Steps

The successful integration of VR/AR into library services requires a multifaceted approach, extending beyond initial implementation. Strategic planning is crucial; it's not enough to simply acquire the technology. A comprehensive assessment of your library's needs, resources, and existing infrastructure is paramount. Consider the specific services you wish to enhance through VR/AR, targeting areas where the technology can demonstrably improve user experience or efficiency. This might involve analyzing patron usage data to identify areas where VR/AR could be most impactful, perhaps guiding the decision to prioritize virtual tours over AR-enhanced book displays, based on demonstrable user demand.

Thorough staff training is non-negotiable. Librarians need to be comfortable and proficient in using the technology, not just as users, but also as instructors and troubleshooters for patrons. Invest in training programs that cover technical aspects, pedagogical strategies for utilizing VR/AR in various library contexts, and effective troubleshooting techniques to address inevitable technical glitches. This requires budgeting for ongoing professional development and potentially partnering with technology providers for tailored training. Consider also peer-to-peer learning opportunities within your library system or regional collaborations.

Cultivating user engagement is key. Don't simply launch VR/AR initiatives and hope for the best. Promote your new services creatively, highlighting their benefits and ease of use through library websites, social media, flyers, and in-person demonstrations. Gather user feedback regularly through surveys, focus groups, or informal feedback mechanisms. This iterative process allows for adjustments to address user needs and preferences. Creating user-friendly interfaces and intuitive navigation within VR/AR environments is pivotal.

Data-driven evaluation is essential to demonstrate the return on investment in VR/AR technologies and to inform future development. Track key metrics, including usage statistics, user satisfaction, and the impact on key library services such as reference assistance or digital literacy program effectiveness. Compare these metrics to pre-implementation data to quantify the impact of VR/AR. This data not only justifies continued investment but also provides crucial evidence for securing funding from external sources, showcasing the tangible value and return of investing in VR/AR technology.

Collaboration is another vital element. Partner with other libraries, educational institutions, technology providers, and community organizations to share best practices, resources, and expertise. Joint projects can reduce costs, accelerate development, and foster innovation. This collaborative approach ensures that your library is part of a broader network leveraging knowledge and experience to overcome challenges and exploit opportunities, maximizing the impact of VR/AR integration and spreading the benefits to a wider community of library users. This might involve sharing of 3D models, collaborative development of AR applications or even joint procurement of equipment.

Finally, consider the long-term sustainability of your VR/AR initiatives. Develop a comprehensive maintenance and update plan for hardware and software, incorporating regular system checks, security protocols, and periodic upgrades. This not only ensures the long-term functionality of your VR/AR infrastructure but also ensures its continued relevance and compatibility with evolving technologies. Budget appropriately for ongoing maintenance and ensure sufficient technical support is available to address technical issues promptly and efficiently. A robust and well-maintained infrastructure is crucial for long-term success.

www.ingramcontent.com/pod-product-compliance
Lightning Source LLC
LaVergne TN
LVHW022026200926
848481LV00007B/2555